T0208206

WHEN
LOVE
is
not
ENOUGH!

WHEN LOVE is not ENOUGH!

JESSICA BARRAGAN

WHEN LOVE IS NOT ENOUGH!

iUniverse books may be ordered through booksellers or by contacting:

iUniverse
1663 Liberty Drive
Bloomington, IN 47403
www.iuniverse.com
1-800-Authors (1-800-288-4677)

Because of the dynamic nature of the Internet, any web addresses or links contained in this book may have changed since publication and may no longer be valid. The views expressed in this work are solely those of the author and do not necessarily reflect the views of the publisher, and the publisher hereby disclaims any responsibility for them.

Any people depicted in stock imagery provided by Getty Images are models, and such images are being used for illustrative purposes only.
Certain stock imagery © Getty Images.

ISBN: 978-1-5320-9253-4 (sc)
ISBN: 978-1-5320-9252-7 (e)

Print information available on the last page.

iUniverse rev. date: 04/07/2020

When Love is Not Enough! Women have unrealistic expectations when it comes to dating a man and marriage. I don't blame women. At a young age, we are taught to fall in love with prince charming and that he's going to make us happy and whole. We are led to believe that men will give us that perfect love. In reality, that mentality only gives us superficial expectations as we get older, and consequently, be disappointed by men. We see it all the time. For example, the girl who falls in love so deeply with her high school sweetheart and gives up her virginity to him. She thought

they'll be together forever only to be cheated on, disappointed and heartbroken. She thinks that if she gives her virginity, heart, loyalty, and love to her "high school sweetheart," that he will reciprocate that back to her as if he's going to admire every good intention that she has towards him and say, "wow, her love don't cost a thing, she's a good woman, she gave up her virginity to me." Instead of experiencing a fairytale love, she is used, heartbroken and left in disappointment in matters of love. As women get older and wiser though, love diminishes and now they start to fall in love with a man's wealth and get married for wealth. Pretty much what she can get out of the marriage rather than love itself. The weakness of a woman is her (heart). She has been taught to be submissive, loyal, and faithful. It pretty much becomes the "proverbs of woman" that the bible speaks of. But that only leaves women in stressful and bad marriages that are more bitter than sweet. Here are a few examples of women I've come across in my lifetime. The woman who falls in love with a convict who is in prison, whom her cousin introduced them both to each other. She paypals him in prison behind her boyfriend's back, that she's living with. She waits on

3

her convict "sancho" to be released from prison so that they can be together at last and live happily ever after. At home, her boyfriend has no idea why she's so cold, distant towards him and why she rejects him sexually. All she wants is for her boyfriend that she is living with to listen to her and to come to an agreement to fix problems, but instead, her husband ignores the issues and problems they have and therefore, she becomes bitter, distant and resents her boyfriend. She has now checked out emotionally and has officially started an emotional affair with this convict who is about to be released from prison and has built a personal attachment with him because "he listens to her problems." She's not really thinking about the consequences of her actions. Here are a few examples. Is she going to get a job to maintain him? Is he going to be a hardworking man? Or is he going to make up plenty of excuses as to why he can't get a job? Or for how long is he going to keep flattering her with lies until he gets what he wants from her only to leave her? Ask yourself, what can this convict bring to your life? Would he make a positive impact upon your life? Ask yourself, is he going to take away from you or add more to you upon your life? Measure the pros and cons. These are

questions that desperate women who are seeking love should ask themselves. Unfortunately, instead of asking these questions, they are going with "the flow." Until, they can't keep up with them anymore. Or how about the woman who has babies from different baby daddies because her high expectations regarding love are not met? She is so disappointed in love, she becomes bitter and at some point even regrets having kids as to say (all this sacrifice and these men don't respect me and are not loyal). She now finds herself in the welfare office applying for food stamps or working at McDonalds trying to make ends meet. The baby daddies aint helping her financially either because she was easy to manipulate through words and lies. (She never tested a man's actions). So they do not respect her and do not even bother paying her child support. To top it off, none of her baby daddies ever married her. So now she doesn't get half their money nor half their assets, not even alimony. All because she believed in these guys and gave her heart wholeheartedly without testing if their words aligned with their actions. Instead of using her brains and utilizing these men financially, her weakness kicks in because of her heart. Now, how about the woman that she

doesn't ask for much in a relationship? In fact, she pays for her meals when she goes on dates with men. The only guy she attracts are men who eventually borrow money from her (without doing that for her in return). He also stays at her apartment and uses her car and decides to quit his job because he takes her kindness for weakness. He also senses low self esteem and knows she craves to be loved. Therefore, he knows that she'll take care of him. This type of woman hardly ever learns her lesson and continues to make the same mistake in giving her all to a man and never puts boundaries with them because she's afraid that they'll reject her. She wasn't taught to self love nor self care for herself. She assumes that whoever she is with in a relationship is supposed to make her happy. She questions herself why she always gets used and cheated on by men. She doesn't realize she has officially taken on the role of a man (being the persuader and chaser) rather than her being persuaded and chased after. She fails to realize that she's more into him rather than him being into her! So now, she is beyond mad, telling all her friends how she "was so good to him" and "wow he took the other woman out to a fine restaurant." Something that he never did with her! So now she hates all

men and says "men aint shit." But instead of learning from her mistakes, she continues to give her loyalty, heart, money, and her time with these broke ass dudes that have nothing to offer her. Or how about the Christian woman who got with the "good ol Christian man" because she thought since "he follows Christ he will only have eyes for her." So they both start courting but eventually are rushed by the church members to "hurry up and marry because they'll be living in sin." This Christian woman doesn't ask for much either. Her only desire is to be loved and for her soon to be husband to be faithful and loyal to her. She thinks love is enough. Love will support marriage itself. They have a small wedding (nothing fancy) and her now Christian husband works a low minimum wage job. Doesn't have any ambition to better his life nor finances. As they move in together, she realizes her husband is not only low libido (with a small penis) but finds out that her husband has a porn addiction and also follows half naked women on social media. She confronts him about this issue, but instead, he tells her "stop being insecure, you shouldn't be insecure because I married you." She is left heartbroken and her expectations of a Godly man are out to the trash. She

regrets marrying this devil in disguise, not only is he a broke ass dude with no motivation, but she's also mad at herself for lowering her standards into thinking that (because he goes to church that he would have eyes only for her and be faithful to her). But in all reality, her expectations of "the perfect man " are nonexisting. She speaks to the pastor about her husband's addiction to pornography only to find out that all the men at that church have the same problem with pornography! So the pastor tells her "pray for your husband's addiction to go away and do a fasting." This only makes her even more angry and she hates her husband. She dislikes when her husband tries to be intimate with her. But now she feels stuck in the marriage. Eventually, she starts seeking her own adventure and meets a hot looking guy at work and soon enough they're off to having an affair. Believe it or not, she is more happy that even her husband is amazed as to why she's more vibrant and happy. However, he doesn't question her whereabouts and is oblivious of what is going on. He has no idea she is having an affair and she is definitely enjoying it! Their marriage has lost communication and they're both living in their own world. Or how about the

woman who helped "build up with her man." She encourages him to finish law school while she drops out of law school herself. She gets a full-time job instead, to help her man pay off his law school debt. She is also pregnant and about to give birth to their baby boy. She makes this sacrifice thinking that they are going to hit it off, get married and that she'll be a stay at home mom while her soon to be husband becomes a lawyer finally. But it all falls apart when he starts working at a law firm. There he meets this beautiful young woman at the law firm. It first starts out innocent. Then the flirting becomes more than just a fling. He tells his baby momma that he is "working long hours at work," but in all reality, he is taking the young mistress to dine and wine. While his baby momma on the other hand, is at home taking care of their 1 week old baby boy. Eventually, she finds out about her man's affair and he tells her he felt stuck with her because of their baby and that he didn't love her anymore. He adds that he is off to make his life with the mistress and marry her. She is left heartbroken and carries resentment towards her man and she is also angry at herself for dropping out of law school to help his ungrateful ass. Love is not enough and women

need to understand that. They have high expectations of what love should be and when their expectations are not met, they are bitter and angry at all the "sacrifices they made" when in all reality, they chose to do that themselves because they thought the men were going to give them the same amount of love, loyalty, and meet their needs in return. Ladies, stop chasing for love because all men cheat. Stop falling in love with men who are broke and are asking you to help build with them. In the end, he will leave you and get with the woman he wanted in the first place. Understand that men also use women for their own benefit and you should use them too. Stop falling for these broke ass cheaters that want you to put 50/50 in the relationship. You're only going to age faster and be stressed all the time. If you don't believe me, look at the women who helped out their man financially. Most of them have let themselves go. They do not wear make -up, they've gained weight, and they complain about how they do not have time for anything (other than work at a shitty ass job that they hate). They gossip and talk crap about the women who are not helping their man financially, who take care of their physical appearance, who go to the gym and care about their looks

and health. Cheating is not always a physical thing but, it is also a mental thing. How do you think affairs start? They meet someone hot online, they send her a message on social media and the men wait to see if the woman is interested in them or not. Then they move on to their next target if they get rejected. Eventually, they butter one of them up. She falls for him, they go out, and they have fun. They go to the nearest motel 6, have sex and there the affair has officially started. Although the mistress has no idea that he is married because he doesn't have any pictures of his wife nor kids on social media. And to top it off he has (single) on his status. Eventually, he gets caught up, his wife finds out about the affair, and tells his wife that he's going to "leave the mistress and that it was a mistake from his part that he cheated on her and that he is sorry." When in reality he is just "sorry" because he got caught. Think about it? If he was sorry in the first place, he wouldn't have done that to begin with. If you didn't bring up his affair he would continue to go along with the affair. So ladies say no to love, get your wealth and eat your cake too. Now, on the other hand, he tells his mistress the same thing he told his wife "I'm going to leave her, I am going to get a divorce

soon just give me time because of the kids." These types of men are up to no good, not even with the most expensive leash and lock because they are cheats and pathological liars. So ladies, stop looking for love and instead start chasing a man's wealth and use it to your advantage and upgrade your lifestyle! Get married for money and not love. You're better off with having stability where you can have the freedom to be a stay at home mom, publish a book, open up your business and know how to utilize his wealth and eat your cake too. But if you get married to a broke ass man that you are taking care of, you're not going to be able to do all that. You won't have the stability because he'll have you working, so you can help him pay half the bills and have more of a roommate type of marriage or relationship. And you don't want that stress upon your shoulders now do you? You want to have the freedom to spend his money, going shopping, getting botox, fillers or even cosmetic surgery. They're many advantages in marrying for wealth, rather than love. It is more beneficial for you. You can choose any career you want and your wealthy husband will pay it for you. It's a win for you and him. How so? Well, he will be constantly chasing after you because you are not into him.

Let me explain, anytime a man gets rejected by the woman he wants he chases after her. Why? Because she's a hard one to catch! He's curious to know why she won't fall for his game (demands). She keeps him wanting for more because she's not predictable, she's not easy to butter her up, she has high expectations and knows exactly what she wants in a man and she's so self confident and assertive she doesn't give a fuck what he thinks of her. He admires how she stands up for herself! She's not messaging him nor picking up his calls the second he calls her. But instead, she calls him whenever she wants, it's not the other way around. She knows when to tease and when to pull away to have him coming for more. Men are the chaser's and the persuaders. They cannot stand the rejection of an attractive, confident woman. That is why wealthy men are attracted to "gold diggers" because they know they ain't getting shit from her unless he drops that cash in return. (I don't want to throw Melanie and Donald Trump as an example here, but , you know what I mean.) Anyway, women who take the role of a man, in persuading a man, in doing everything for their man, the only thing they get out of it is their man taking advantage of them and demanding even more from their

woman. You see the more you do for a man the more lazy he becomes. Why? Because you're doing everything for him. You're not even letting him be a man. You're not letting him chase after you anymore. He doesn't even have to marry you nor put a ring on it, why? Because you already gave him kids, you gave him the wifey duties without even being married to him. You already cook, clean and do his laundry for free. Why pay? When he can get the cow for free. Why should he make an effort now? When you easily gave him access to your entire being without asking him for shit in return. But now all of a sudden, it bothers you and you complain to your girlfriends how your man "ain't doing shit for you, when he never did shit for you to begin with? Because you never set the boundaries in the first place. Especially, if you were seeking more than just a one night stand. But now you're heartbroken and in shock why he didn't change for you? Some women are taught to settle for anything and any man without questioning their motives. That is why some women are stuck in toxic relationships. But If the woman has a list of expectations she is called selfish, golddigger, unrealistic, shallow, etc. But men do it all the time! They always want the best

looking woman and expect for them to lower their standards. If not, they get mad when they get rejected and if she explains to him her expectations, he is somehow bothered and belittles her. And the men that are married follow all these instagram models with big asses, tiny waists and big breasts. They are somehow ashamed of their wives because they've gained weight after having kids. They want them to look like those models but don't want to pay for their wife to hire a personal trainer so they can get back in shape. But they're not willing to pay for them to get the "mommy make-over cosmetic procedure). Some husbands don't even want to have sex with their wife anymore because they are insulted and grossed the fuck out of the scar and loose skin of her stomach after she had a c-section! (Hello! Your baby's umbilical cord was around your baby's neck!) Or how about husbands who have tons of excuses why they can't babysit either, because "they're too tired from work." But they're not too tired to follow half naked women and giving likes on Instagram or ever too tired to jerk off to pornography, right? Now, let's bring back the Christian women, whom during my lifetime tried to give me advice! But couldn't help themselves out nor take their

own advice. How sad and bitter most of them really are. They are taught not to wear make-up. Or how about the dress code? Long dresses that make them look like a nun. They are taught to neglect themselves, to be the sacrifice of their husband when they cheat (to pray for them). When their husband cheats on them and gets caught. They blame their wife. They make the excuse that the reason they cheated was because, "she let herself go, she doesn't spend time with him anymore, or she changed a lot." Well no fucking shit! Let's see here, she gets up in the morning to make breakfast for you and the kids. She gets her kids ready for school. She comes home, cleans after all of you (including you, the husband who throws your boxer briefs on the floor, when there's two laundry baskets! You watch the basketball game most of the time and you can't even aim at both laundry baskets to put your laundry)? And how about that in most churches the woman needs to forgive and forget her cheating husband's sexual escapades with hookers, strippers and prostitutes?

Because after all, when she got married she accepted for "good and bad till death do us apart type of bullshit." So she's stuck in a sad and bitter marriage. He also makes his

kids go to church and how to dress modestly. He teaches them what is good and bad according to his bullshit. But he doesn't follow none of what he "teaches his kids nor puts it into practice himself!" At home, he doesn't tell his wife that she's beautiful, but instead, he criticizes her weight and looks. And when she finally speaks her mind, lo and behold! He tells her to be quiet! And how she must submit and be obedient to him because he's "the man of the household." So in all this, this religious husband has a double life! He wants a proverb woman but has a weakness for a harlot or Jezebel woman. At church, he is respected and people in the congregation speak good things about him. He is very kind and in fact likes to help his fellow members at his church a lot. And his wife is quiet and she doesn't participate much in the conversations because she was taught to be silent. But when it's time to go home, his kind, generous, loving, and caring demeanor changes completely to the devil himself. Even his own kids dislike him and have caught on to their father's bullshit. For the church members, this family seems to be perfect as they also dress very modestly. But little do they know they live in the devil's playground with a dictator who has no solid

foundation of what love truly is. And uses bible verses to his advantage and what is only beneficial for him. Most women have good intentions and never want to "hurt" anyone and only get played. They are still in the (innocent mindset). That somehow, what they give, they must also receive from the men in return. The same amount of love, care, loyalty and so forth. You must understand this world has two types of people, good and evil. You're either the predator or the victim. There is no in between, no rules, when it comes to love. You play at your own risk, you allow how you get treated and what you want out of this life. You're better off making the best of it and play the game. So learn to detach emotionally and never show your vulnerability to a man. Never confide your most intimate moments with him either. Don't give them your 100% loyalty because the truth is, you're not going to get that in return. If you are skeptical about this try by testing him. Make something up that is vulnerable to you and watch him use that against you when he is mad. I've heard so many times of women who allowed their man to know their vulnerability only so that he uses their vulnerability against them sooner rather than later. I heard a man speak about his girlfriend of 24 years into

their relationship about how if it wasn't for him, she'll still be eating food from the dumpster. How she grew up poor and how her parents never loved her and how if it wasn't for him getting her out of her household, that she would never find anyone that "loved her more than he does." He was definitely speaking ill things about her and was proud of it. As you can see, he also never married her. They've been together for over 24 years. I can imagine the manipulation tactics that he pulls on her. I am convinced that he uses her vulnerability against her more than once to have control over her. Women have to learn when to become the damsel in distress depending on the situation and how to do it the right way, to get the right results. If they want to gain money and wealth from them in return, women need to start off by loving themselves again and build up their confidence. Remember how you used to love dressing up and how you couldn't leave the house without first putting on your make-up on? Look at yourself in the mirror and tell yourself that, "you are beautiful, you are smart, and that your purpose in life is greater than mediocrity. Tell yourself that you deserve the best in this world. Remember the great things you loved doing before you even met him?

Remember how you loved painting before you even met him but you stopped because you got married to him and you placed him first upon your life? So slowly without you even noticing it, you lost yourself and your woman power (confidence). Start going to the gym and get back in shape. Not only are you going to feel better about yourself, but your health is also going to improve. The first step is to take action so do not think about it, just do it! The second you start thinking about if you should rise up and go to the gym or decide to hit the snooze button and go back to sleep, is when you have lost. Don't make excuses as to why you cannot go to the gym today or workout. But rather make an effort, even if you can't afford to go to the gym. There's plenty of options, a quick work out at your nearest park or even at your back yard! So no excuses! Set up a schedule and stick to it. Finally, do not tell anyone your plans or goals for this year. Some people don't have the best intentions upon your life and will only try to sabotage or bring you down about your goals so at the end, you get discouraged and won't get shit done. You know exactly who they are! These can be your family members, friends, co-workers, even a spouse! They don't understand that

everyone has their own unique persona and purpose in life, so don't get discouraged by them and believe in yourself. You can achieve what you set your mind to! So, no matter what, stick to your goals, tackle them and achieve them one by one. The reason for not telling is because not everyone understands your journey. You are authentic, you are not them. But if you're dying to tell them, at least wait after you achieve them. Not everyone wants to see you succeed in life, especially when you're doing better than them! They will try to bring you down because they themselves feel that they have nothing going on in their lives and are not happy with themselves. So these (dream killers) will stop at nothing to keep you in their misery web if you allow them. Start gaining your confidence back and start self healing and forgiving yourself for all the past mistakes you've made in the past. Block all your exes from social media, forgive them also, and move on. You have gotten used to being single and you are now confident going out. You have taken care of your appearance and have hit the gym. You are looking like a diva everytime you leave the house. You have officially achieved the level up process. Congratulations to the new and improved you! You know

exactly what you want in a man now and you're sticking to your needs and wants. You're not one for compromise any longer nor downgrade your standards anymore. You've come a long way to find the real you, who is the best you! Now it's game time! Get out there and play! This book is dedicated to all the women from all over the world. Who went through a lot of shit and felt they couldn't say shit for whatever reason. For the women whom I was surrounded by in my lifetime. For all ya who told me to shut the fuck up, and let God take care of it. Big shout out to Noemi for being a great friend to me and believing in me. Also, Steven who always has my back. You've told me to speak my mind so here it is! Ha!__

This book is dedicated to all the women from all over the world. Who went through a lot of shit and felt they couldn't say shit for whatever reason. For the women whom I was surrounded by in my lifetime. For all ya who told me to shut the fuck up, and let God take care of it. Big shout out to Noemi for being a great friend to me and believing in me. Also, Steven who always has my back. You've told me to speak my mind so here it is! Ha!

Printed in the United States
By Bookmasters